Cover image
"the Peabody River"

Dolly Emery Copp

DOLLY COPP

AND

THE PIONEERS OF

THE GLEN

by
George N. Cross

SicPress 2013
Methuen, Mass.

George N. Cross's *Dolly Copp and the Pioneers of the Glen* was originally published in 1927. Cross is the author of *Randolph old and new : its ways and its by-ways* and *My Childhood in Pleasant Valley* published in 2012 by SicPress.

Cover image: "Peabody River."

©2013, SicPress.com
14 Pleasant St.
Methuen, Massachusetts.
sales@sicpress.com

"We take up the task eternal,
and the burden and the lesson,
Pioneers! O Pioneers!"

Walt Whitman

⑦OLLY ⓒⓄOPP

AND THE PIONEERS OF THE GLEN

"ⓌHO WAS DOLLY COPP?" — hundreds of people this year, just as did hundreds last year, will ask as they park their cars, pitch their tents, kindle their camp fires under the blue dome of the great out of doors at Dolly Copp Camp in the Glen in the White Mountains.

Come with me a few rods along the Randolph road from Dolly Copp Bridge to a point where close to the road a widespreading butternut tree casts its shade over the scattered foundation stones of an old farm house. Here is the spot and here I will tell you a story of pioneer heroism as absorbing as a Leatherstocking tale. There are no Indians in the story. But in every other respect it is the equal of the annals of the Pilgrims of Plymouth.

To begin at the beginning—in the days of the French and Indian wars Thomas Martin served the English Crown so faithfully as a purchaser of military stores for the British army that King George III, in 1775, deeded to him a tract of land right here in the Glen along the banks of the Peabody River. This tract came to be known as Martin's Location. South of this Location was a smaller tract known as Green's Grant. For sixty years these two tracts of virgin forest, filling the valley and climbing the slopes on either side of the Glen, were an unexplored wilderness, the haunt of the bear, the wolf, the wildcat and the deer. In 1834 a pioneer by the name of Hadley bought Green's Grant for five hundred dollars. There is no evidence, however, that the new purchaser ever made any use of his possession.

In 1790 Captain Joseph Pinkham of Madbury, New Hampshire with four neighboring families, migrated to rich lands on the lower part of the Ellis River. It was in the month of April. But the hard-frozen snow lay five feet deep along their route. In the party was a young son of Captain Pinkham, Daniel, ten years old, lively and resourceful. The flocks and herds that usually were driven along with migrating trains were represented by a single young pig. This pig the boy taught to work in harness and draw over the frozen snow the sled on which were lashed the few household goods. The place where they settled they named New Madbury, which in time grew to be beautiful Jackson.

In 1804, in the town of Stowe, Maine, not far from the New Hampshire line, was born Hayes Dodifer Copp. Before he was twenty years of age he had found his way through Fryeburg to the prosperous communities of Bartlett and Jackson. There he heard of a forest Eldorado twenty miles from Jackson, up in the heart of the White Hills, where gold was to be extracted from black soil with axe and torch and ploughshare.

Young Copp entered into negotiations with the New Hampshire Legislature and obtained a deed of a future farm in the forest lands of Martin's Location. In place of money, for the boy possessed not a copper, he pledged himself to pay for his farm in wheat, barley and oats, which he would raise on his land after he had made it ready for crops. After years of toil Copp paid this debt to the last bushel.

So a hundred years ago, in 1827, as near as very meagre records will allow us to fix a date, Hayes D. Copp, twenty-four years of age, small of stature, shoulders already bent with toil, a shapely head under a curling shock of yellow hair, pale blue eyes, a sound heart well stored with pluck and grit, a small pack on his back, his long-barreled flintlock gun over his shoulder, his axe in his hand, set out to locate and make his farm.

A blazed trail followed the Ellis up what is now Pinkham Notch and down the Peabody, crossing the stream where now is Dolly Copp Bridge. This was the pioneer's route. Somehow, somewhere on the trunks of great trees he found the surveyors' marks that told him the land the legislature had sold him lay along the alluvial levels on the river bank and up the slopes of Madison.

Imagination and the experiences related in the few letters of earlier pioneers in the White Mountains alone can tell the story of Hayes Copp's first years of struggle to hew a farm and home out of the savage wilderness of the Glen. His first care was a shelter, a lean-to of poles, roofed and enclosed on three sides with strips of hemlock bark. In front of the open side of the shelter he built a fireplace of flat stones on which to cook his food. For food the river and every brook swarmed with trout, bears crashed through the berry thickets, morning and evening deer came down to the river to drink, grouse drummed on the prostrate logs, pigeons roosted in the branches over his head. On his occasional trips to Jackson he obtained pork, Indian meal and salt. From the disappearance of the snow in spring to its coming again in the early winter, the

8

Hayes Dodifer Copp

days of the short summer were filled with grinding toil, felling, piling, burning the great trees. In the second spring he "scratched in" round the blackened stumps in his little clearing turnip and pumpkin seeds and perhaps a few patches of wheat. The 'black soil, the humus of ages of fallen leaves, awoke in the sunshine and gave the toiler a harvest.

On the spot now shaded by the butternut by the road- side Hayes "rolled up" a one-room log cabin, and, a little nearer the river, a log barn for the shelter of the sheep and cows that were so-on to be bought. It would seem that Hayes Copp must have given from three to five years of his young life to forcing the savagery of the Glen to yield to civilization and grant to him the reward of a farm and home. Then, he was ready for a helpmate.

Some time, perhaps on one of his rare visits to Jackson and Bartlett, Hayes had met Dolly Emery, a girl just his own age, small in stature, with flaxen hair and light blue eyes that had a flash of keenness. Dolly was possessed, too, with a very glib tongue. The pioneer had scant time for courtship, and the wooing was doubtless brief.

Hayes Copp and Dolly Emery were married in Bartlett November 3, 1831. From hints and scraps gathered from many sources we can piece together a tolerably accurate story of Dolly's wedding journey and the early days of her married life.

The bride doubtless rode upon the back of a sturdy horse, which also drew the bridal "car." This simple vehicle consisted of two long birch poles, the smaller ends of which served as thills between which the horse was harnessed. The larger ends of the two poles trailed along the ground behind like sled runners. Two cross pieces were pinned to the runner about three feet apart and completed the framework of the sled. To the sled were lashed a few household utensils and a small box or leathern trunk containing the bride's trousseau. Of the possible contents of that trunk we may learn a little more later. Now we may see only a pair of dainty shoes. Dolly had very small feet, of which she was inordinately proud. In all her married life, while she made with her own hands every other article of her apparel, she always sent to Portland for her shoes.

Hayes walks beside the horse, carrying over his shoulder his long - barreled gun, not for protection, for few dangers lurk along their path, but to add to their larder the grouse that may scurry or the deer that may leap across their path.

So almost a hundred years ago Hayes and Dolly Copp, winding in and out among the blazed trees, journeyed up the Ellis and down the Peabody, along the Glen to the blackened clearing and the cabin home where they were to toil together for fifty years to wrest from the forest the sunny fields, the fruitful orchard where now each summer thousands of tourists from many lands pitch their tents to find vacation joy in the open.

The Copps were to live their lives of neighborless isolation fewer years, perhaps, than they had anticipated.

In 1824 Durand, six miles beyond the mountain wall to the west, became the incorporated town of Randolph, with a growing community of farmers and

The Copp Farmhouse

lumbermen. Jackson, twelve miles to the south, with rich lands and a promise 0-f mining wealth, was becoming important. Early in the decade of the thirties the legislature of New Hampshire contracted with Daniel Pinkham to build a graded wagon road along the old blazed trail to connect Jackson and Randolph. It was a work of several years, with few avail able laborers and few tools. But the pluck and resourcefulness of the man who, in his boyhood, had taught his pig to draw his sled, accomplished it. Daniel Pinkham received a grant of land on both sides of his road, which gave the name to Pinkham Notch. So the Copps early found their settlers' home close beside a highway that was to be more- and more frequently traveled. They set themselves to their task of years and years as only a man and woman of perfect health, great strength and indomitable will can work in living conditions of bracing air, sparkling waters, simple, strong food, in one of the loveliest spots towering mountains ever looked down upon.

But they needed all their strength and pluck to fight the bears from the young lambs in spring, the wolves from the young cattle in the fall, the foxes, coons and skunks from the poultry yards, the deer from the ripening grain. They must expect the late and early frosts of the too-short summers. They must face the intense cold, terrific winds and deep snows of the always long winters. And they well knew that every year the fight with some of these enemies would be a losing battle.

Each year they enlarged their clearing. Larger fields gave ampler harvests. In spite of bears, wolves and bobcats, the flocks gave their increase. The one-room log cabin gave place to a long, low, frame house, neatly painted and

11

connected by an ell with a roomy frame barn between the highway and the river. These buildings were standing within the memory of the writer.

In all this struggle of fifty years Dolly Copp's strength and energy kept pace with her ambition. Her hands performed a. thousand tasks of which the modern housekeeper has no knowledge. In the spring she saw to the setting of the hens and raised fine brood of chickens. She helped Hayes shear the sheep, cleansed and carded the wool, spun the snowy rolls into yarn, wove the yarn on her clumsy loom into cloth or knit it into socks for the whole family. In the corner of the ell room stood the brass kettle in which in the fall she made hundreds of "tallow dips." Ranged along the barnyard wall were the barrels and tubs, and the kettle swung over the outdoor fireplace where in the early spring she made the

year's supply of soap. In the winter evenings, by the light of her tallow dips burning on the light stand before the fireplace, she knit or darned, made or mended the garments of the whole family.

There is a tradition of Gorham that Joseph Jackson brought on his back from Canterbury, New Hampshire, a sackful of little apple trees to grow into the first apple orchard in Shelbourne Addition. As you wander about the old Copp farm today you will note the rows of gnarled, decaying tree trunks where Dolly had her fine apple orchard behind the house. She began her orchard not many years after Joseph Jackson planted his first trees in Gorham. But she did not import her trees from some distant town. She searched through the woods and along the river bank for the "Johnny Apple Seed" trees that grow everywhere. Promising trees she transplanted in her orchard. The "wildings" responded to constant care and cultivation, grew to great size and bore apples of fine varieties.

For forty years the Pinkham Notch road was the one highway between Jackson and Randolph and the north country, and the Copp home the one large dwelling between those places. Although it was never licensed as such, it naturally became a sort of tavern. Travelers in either direction usually stopped for a meal, or, if they arrived late, spent the night. Dolly's good food and comfortable beds became widely known. The price of entertainment was not exorbitant—"a shilling all round," that is, twenty-five cents for a meal, the same for a bed for each person and a quarter for the feed and care of a horse.

From the vivid memory of some of Dolly's long-ago guests still living it is possible to make a tolerably accurate pen picture of the Copp home and its mistress. By a door on the south side of the house the traveler entered the living room, a large, low, square apartment. Opposite the door was a huge stone fireplace, in which usually blazed a hospitable tire. In the corner at the right stood a rude wooden loom and beside it a large spinning wheel; in the corner at the left a wide bed, covered with a hand-woven, light blue coverlet. Near the fireplace ticked a "grandfather's" clock, the early history of which Dolly has herself handed down to us. The ancient timepiece is still preserved in one of the homes of Gorham. On the inside of the case is this curious little memorandum in Dolly's quaint and odd hand:

"In the year of 1821 there were twelve of these clocks brought into the town of Jackson, State of New Hampshire, and sold for twenty dollars. I bought this one of Capt. Anthony Vinson [Vincent], who then lived on what was afterward called the Carlton place, in Randolph. It was forty-eight years ago last September that I bought it and paid five and one-half dollars for it. It was for many years an excellent timekeeper.

Over the fireplace on wooden pins hung two long-barreled guns, one of them with a flint lock. Around the room stood several splint-bottomed chairs. From a crane a teakettle was suspended over the fire, and on a flat stone in front of it stood a frying pan and a tin baker.

In cold weather this living room served as kitchen and dining room also. The late Eugene B. Cook of Hoboken, who was once a storm-bound guest over night at the Copp farm, gave the writer many years ago a vivid description of Dolly's table as it was spread for supper before the fire. Of the food served that night Mr. Cook could remember nothing but that it was a very satisfying supper for a tired and hungry tramper. He recalled that the table was covered with a snowy, fringed linen cover that would make you modern housewives draw a long breath. Dolly raised the flax in the narrow flax field by the river, pulled and heckled the flax, spun it on the small flax wheel as she rocked Sylvia's cradle, wove it on the loom in the corner and bleached it in the sun and dew of the orchard behind the house. The table was resplendent with a silver teapot and sugar bowl, and delicate china ornamented with a narrow gilt band and tiny flowers. Of the silver pieces Dolly was frankly very proud. They were probably heirlooms, and as a part of the bridal outfit had come up the trail lashed to the bridal car. In Dolly's heart, beneath the toil-worn exterior of the pioneer, lived the woman's love of the refined and beautiful.

On the right of the fireplace was the huge brick oven of olden times in which each Saturday morning a fire was built. When it was hot the coals were raked out and the floor swept clean with an oven broom. Into the cavernous depths, with a long, pronged hook, were pushed a roast of pork, or venison, or bear, a pot of pork and beans, another of Indian pudding, and other delicacies of the pioneer's table. The oven was then sealed with a heavy wooden shutter and the savory viands left to simmer all night in the mellow heat and be drawn forth in the morning, a Sunday breakfast for a sturdy, hungry family.

At the foot of the bed stood a heavy wooden cradle painted red and furnished with a hand-woven coverlet of the same light blue as the one on the larger bed. Into that cradle in 1832 came Jeremiah, to grow up a stalwart son, a cheerful helper in every task of the farm, skilled in all the arts of forest and stream. In later years Jerry married and removed to Littleton, where he lived to a goodly age, famed as the most skilful trout fisherman in all the region. He died in Meredith in 1910.

In a year Jerry had to yield the warm, red cradle to baby Nat. Of Nathaniel's young manhood of great strength, courage and endurance there will be much to tell presently.

Five years later Dolly rocked in the little red cradle Sylvia, little Sylvia, the fittingly named joy of that woodland-girdled home, the one sweet and gentle element of that stern household. After ten years of rest in the attic the red cradle once more took its accustomed place at the foot of the bed to welcome Daniel, the last baby of the family.

Dolly makes a pleasant picture as she sits by the foot of the bed, one small foot resting on the cradle rocker, and occasionally gently nudging Dan's uneasy slumber, the other foot on the treadle of the flying flax wheel, her deft fingers drawing out the smooth, even linen thread. To be sure, twenty years of never-relaxing toil have wrought changes in the once girlish form — shoulders bent, figure stouter, face pinched and seamed with lines of care, the curly, flaxen hair replaced by a frowsy wig, contentment shining from her pale blue eyes, save an occasional flash of impatience in response to the angry snarl of the tangled wheel.

She is dressed in a gown of pale blue homespun, woven from the wool of her own flock, the plain, loose-fitting garment made by her own hands. It is fastened at the throat with a large, gold breastpin. Her sole other adornment is a necklace of gold beads, bright with years of wear and nervous fingering. Between the lips of her small, firm mouth is held a short-stemmed clay pipe, the comfort and solace of many toilsome hours. Such was Dolly Copp, a typical pioneer woman of the wilderness of Martin's Location seventy-five years ago.

With the years following 1850 it was manifest the clouds which for many years had hung heavy over the Glen were breaking. Brighter days were coming to Hayes and Dolly. A quarter of a mile along the Randolph road, beyond the site of the Copp buildings, you will find traces of a house and barn. Hither a little later than 1850 came a family of English descent by the name of Barnes, to build up a prosperous farm. Not long after Patrick Culhane took up a claim about midway between the Copp and Barnes farms. Across the river, in Green's Grant, had settled Frederick and Sally Spaulding, with their four lively children, Reuben, Sarah, Edwin and Fred, a little older than the Copp children. After so many years of neighborless isolation they were to know neighbors and human friendship. In 1836 Shelbourne Addition became the prosperous and growing town of Gorham. The trail up the Peabody was made a good wagon road connecting with the Pinkham Notch road at the Copp farm. Where now a

14

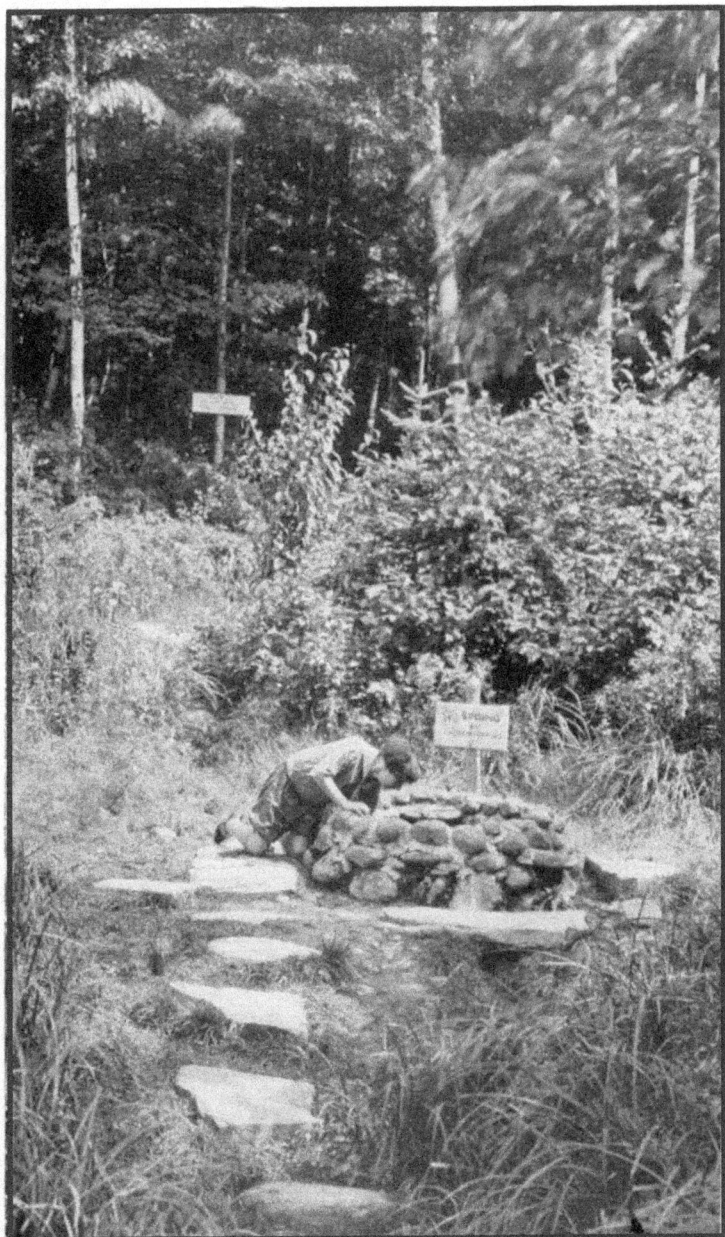

The Dolly Copp Spring

15

substantial iron bridge spans the river, Daniel Pinkham built a low bridge of logs. This frail structure and many of its successors went down the stream in spring freshets. In the long bridgeless intervals travelers were forced to resort to a precarious ford. One of the writer's earliest recollections of the region is of a voyage across this ford in a light Concord wagon, the pilot, Mr. Laban Watson, of Randolph, our frail bark pitching at every possible and frightful angle as the wheels rolled over the huge boulders in the swirling waters, and the horse struggled for the opposite shore.

When a railroad came to Gorham on one side and to Conway on the other, daily mail coaches were put on running through the Glen to connect these two points. Came in 1852 John Bellows, a man of vision, to see future harvests in the sublimity of the mountain tops, the grandeur of the ravines. In the spring of that year Mr. Bellows began the erection of a small hotel on the splendid site that for seventy-five years has been the home of successive Glen Houses.

Keen-eyed Dolly quickly saw the significance of the coming of the "city folks/' It is known that throughout all the years when Dolly was mine hostess to the travelers on the Pinkham Notch road, she entered the names of all her guests in a little blank book. How much of interest concerning the olden ways and golden days in the Glen might be learned if we could find that ancient register!

Dolly early won fame for her handicraft. No other housewife wove so many bolts of woolen homespun, so many yards of linen, could match her dyes of delicate blue, could rival her golden butter, rich cheese and maple syrup. And they all found a market at the Glen House. City folks came to the Copp farm to find how delightful were vacation days spent there, and to return summer after summer.

In the summer of 1874 there came to the farm a mature, refined young woman from Oberlin, Ohio, to find restored health and to stay on till winter snows clothed the Glen.

"From school and ball and rout she came,
The city's fair pale daughter,
To drink the wine of mountain air—"

Daniel was then a ruddy-faced, broad-shouldered, presentable young fellow of twenty-five. It needed only moonlit rambles along the river bank, firelit chats in the living room in autumn, for Lizzie Drew to learn that,

"Nor frock nor tan can hide the man."

From the town records of Gorham we learn that on the 18th of December of that year Daniel Copp and Lizzie Drew were married by the Reverend J. A. Hawkes. The aged minister used to recall that Dolly came along to witness the happy ceremony and offer earliest congratulations. The young couple removed to the bride's home in Oberlin, where they lived many years.

But, if the summers were growing brighter and happier, the winters were still hard and cruel in Martin's Location. Intense cold, terrific winds, mountainous snow banks, wolves skulking in the edge of the clearing, wildcats prowling in the orchard, made all out-of-doors a battlefield. The winter of 1859 the Copps remembered as one of exceptional severity. The second son, Nathaniel, now twenty-four years of age, of iron muscle and indomitable pluck, was always ready to brave the winter's terrors on long hunting trips. In January there came a deep fall of soft, yielding snow. For four successive days Nat was out in the forest from long before light till late in the evening, hunting deer. Very early on the morning of the fifth day he was on his snowshoes, tramping to a point where the day before, just at nightfall, he had shot a deer. He found the animal and dragged the body, weighing 256 pounds, eight miles through the yielding snow. Two miles from home he noticed fresh deer tracks as he passed. Arriving home at 1 o'clock, without waiting for a moment's rest or stopping for food or drink or matches, or even for his gun (for he knew that no gun was needed on that hunt), armed only with his long hunting knife, he eagerly retraced his steps. He found the new track and followed it through the snow-encumbered woods. When darkness descended he could no longer follow the deer; and, worse, he found he had lost all knowledge of his own whereabouts. For a minute of bewilderment he was at a standstill.

Just at that time some one of the family at home noticed that the mercury stood at 34 degrees below zero. Nat's hesitation was for but a moment. He knew there was but one thing to do—to keep moving, somehow, in some direction, to keep his sluggish blood from congealing in his shrinking veins lest he sink down in the snow in that stupor from which there is no waking. And keep moving he did, stumbling on and on for hours through the darkness. After five or six hours the moon came up to afford him its cheering, if unwarming, light. Presently he heard a deer floundering on before him. The sound set his heart beating fast, the blood coursing along his veins. His snowshoes enabled him to quickly overtake the wallowing animal. He then leaped upon its back and cut its throat with his long knife and dressed it.

Aided a little by the light of the moon, the young man again took up his terrible march over frozen brooks, through snow-clogged ravines, stumbling on and on, he knew not whither. Morning and daylight came to find him with strength enough to still stagger on. At 10 o'clock he emerged from the woods at a point on the Wild River, in the village of Gilead, Maine, guided his reeling steps to a house, told his half-coherent story and was put to bed.

The lad had walked on his snowshoes continuously for twenty-one hours, had covered more than forty terrible miles, had kept up an incredible toil for twenty-six hours without food or drink or rest.

Meanwhile at home, as the afternoon wore on toward darkness and a night of frightful cold and Nat did not return, the family became thoroughly alarmed. There was but one thing to do—to go in search of him. Hayes Copp hastened to the nearest neighbors and gave the alarm. Thomas Culhane and his hired man, John Golding, at once volunteered for the rescue. Taking with them two great wolfhounds, they set out, found the young man's track and followed it to the point where he had killed and dressed the deer. By this time darkness had settled over the woods, making it impossible to follow the hunter's trail any farther. So there they built a fire and sat down by it to wait six anxious hours till the coming up of the moon. By the dim light of the waning moon they again set out along Nat's devious, zigzagging track, every moment fearing to come upon his lifeless, frozen body.

Late the next afternoon, after twenty hours of that struggle and racking suspense, the three men reached Gilead village, to be told that Nat was safe and to be led to his bedside. They found him delirious and with both legs so frozen he did not walk a step for six months. Hayes Copp and Thomas Culhane suffered all the rest of their lives from the effects of frostbitten ears, and John Gilding underwent the amputation of both feet.

Such were the heroism and hardihood of the pioneers of the Glen only seventy years ago. And yet were any of those men alive today they would declare, as did Nat Copp again and again to questioning and admiring summer people: "We did nothing remarkable or deserving of any praise."

From 1853 the prospect was ever widening and brightening for the first dwellers in the Glen. Mr. J. M. Thompson had succeeded Mr. Bellows, the founder of the Glen House. This hostelry, small at first, to be sure, yet accessible to the summits and ravines of the great Presidential Range, grew rapidly in popularity and accommodations under the management of this genial, mountain-loving landlord till his death, by drowning, in the Pea-body in 1859. The house demanded more and more of the products of Dolly's skilful hands, and filled those eager hands with ready money.

A widespread belief became current that the one perfect view of the satanic profile then becoming known as "Dolly Copp's Camp' was to be had in the dooryard of the Copp farm. Starr King so declared it in his "White Hills." Samuel Adams Drake, some years later, reiterated the perfection of that particular view. So the great six-horse stages, as they rolled along the Glen road, laden inside and out with eager sightseeing city folks, usually turned aside, crossed the river and drew up beside the Copp home. There the smartly-dressed vacationers divided their interest between Dolly's Imp, standing out clear against a screen of white cloud, and Dolly herself and her modest family gathered shyly about, the father with his pinched face wearing the grim smile of years of endurance, Dolly standing in the doorway, clad in her pale blue dress of homespun, nervously fingering her gold beads, pretty Sylvia shyly peering out over her mother's shoulder, small Daniel clinging to his mother's skirt, Jerry and Nat modestly answering a babel of questions. And thus the name and modest fame of Dolly Copp and her family began to go forth on the lips of the city folks all over New England and far beyond.

In the census of Martin's Location taken in 1850 both Jerry and Nat gave their employment not as farmers but as laborers, making it evident it was their intention, as they did a few years later, to leave the farm. But the opportunity they would seek elsewhere was coming to them right at home. In the summer of 1853, at the Alpine House, in Gorham, a stock company was organized to build a carriage road from the Glen House to the summit of Mount Washington, an enterprise that would prove of great advantage to the Glen.

The construction of those eight difficult miles of good road would employ many men for years. Every detail of the undertaking was doubtless discussed at the family and neighborhood gatherings at the Copp fireside. The model of a carriage to be used on the road had been sent to the Glen House, and, no doubt, came in for a full measure of discussion in that circle. The model was of an omnibus, to be drawn by four horses and to carry twelve passengers. There was a separate seat for each passenger which was placed diagonally, so that the occupant faced neither his opposite nor front nor back, but had an unobstructed view in every direction. The car raige body was so adjusted that the rear end could be raised in ascending and the front end in descending the mountain, so that the carriage floor would be constantly level. There were powerful brakes to be applied to the wheels and to be operated by the feet of the driver. A strap lay along the floor of the carriage which could be pulled by any passenger if necessary and the horses instantly brought to a standstill. Needless to say, this remarkable "omnibus" was never used or even built.

For a year and a half this projected road made progress only on paper and in models. But in 1855 ground was broken and the work carried forward for two years, in which time the road was finely graded and finished as far as the present Cape Horn. While there is no record of it, there is little doubt that some of the Copp menfolks had their share in the big job.

After four miles of the road had been successfully completed, but at a cost far greater than the first estimates, the construction company failed. Through some years of discouragement the enterprise waited for the formation of a new company with sufficient capital to carry the road to the summit, which was triumphantly done in 1861.

And so the years came and went in the busy life of Dolly Copp and her family, the summers brightened by the presence of more and more city folks, the winters mitigated by more comforts in doors and out. The year 1858 was made notable by the severing of hitherto unbroken family ties. In January Jeremiah married Susan Rogers and removed from the farm and the Glen. Late in the autumn Sylvia, a beautiful girl of nineteen, married Benjamin Potter and went to Auburn, Maine, there to make a home to which to welcome Dolly after many years.

The record of Nathaniel's maturer years is difficult to trace. Perhaps to him "Denmark's a prison place."

The mountains may have seemed prison walls. For many years he was a wanderer. In 1860 he married Esther Willey of Gorham and apparently soon after disappeared and Martin's Location knew nothing of him for years. We get glimpses of him seeing the great world as an employee of a circus, then living for some years in Toledo Ohio. Some-what earlier than 1885, he had come home to the Glen and the old farm. After the sale of the homestead Nat became again a homeless wanderer and lived his last aimless years in Brunswick, Maine.

Of Daniel's romance and happy marriage with Lizzie Drew, in 1874, I have earlier told the story.

So, through storm and sunshine, winter's terrors and summer's joys, pinching poverty and substantial comfort, passed fifty years of the married life of Hayes and Dolly Copp.

The annals of New England and family life record not another so strange a Golden Jubilee. Then it was that Dolly said: "Hayes is well enough. But fifty years is long enough for a woman to live with any man."

Peacefully, scrupulously, they divided between them the savings of a lifetime, leaving the old home, leaving the fields, the orchard, the garden, they had made together, they separated, went their chosen ways, Hayes back to his native town of Stowe, Dolly to find a home with her daughter Sylvia, in Auburn, Maine. There, far from each other, far from the scenes of their life work, they lived their remaining years.

* * *

In 1885 Nathaniel sold the farm to E. Libby and Sons and went away from the Glen. Sylvia Copp Potter, at the goodly age of eighty-nine years, is still living (1927) in Auburn, cherishing happy memories of her girlhood days in Glen Peabody.

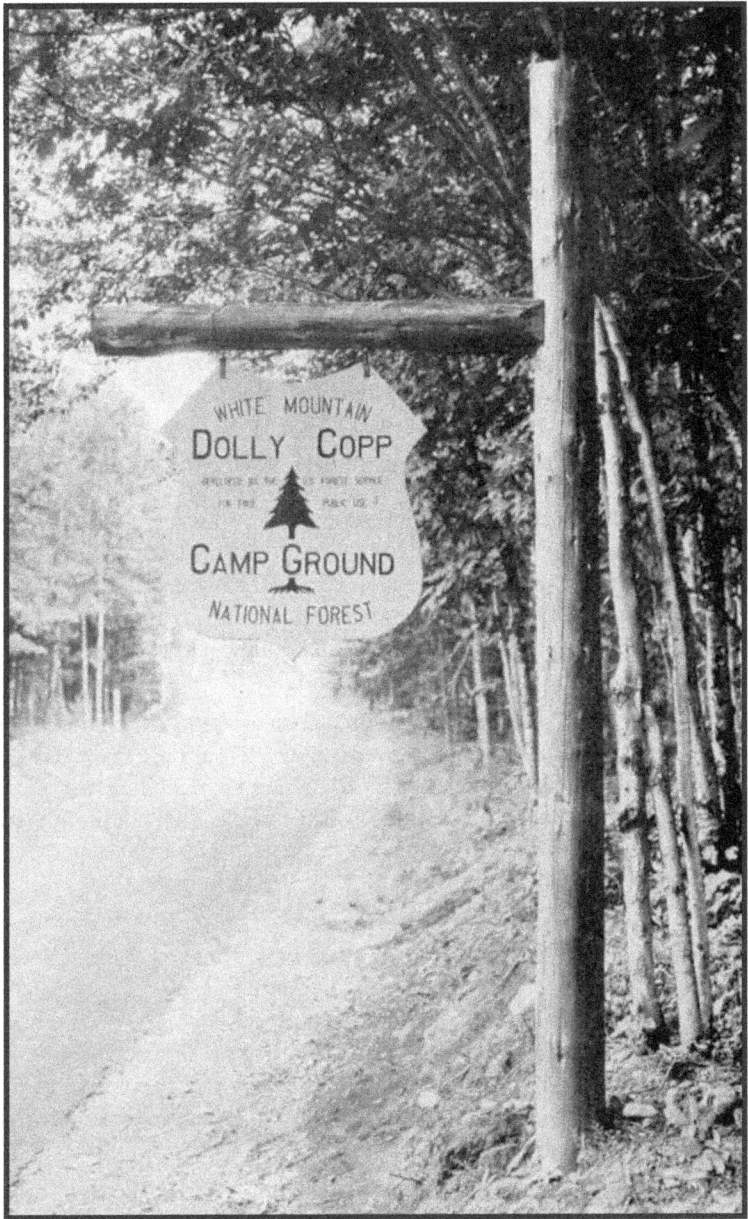

WHITE MOUNTAIN
DOLLY COPP

CAMP GROUND

NATIONAL FOREST

THE MOTOR CAR COMES TO THE GLEN

Very early on the morning of Sunday, August 31, 1899, a farmer on the Randolph road was seen hurrying across his dooryard to the cottage of a summer neighbor, in great excitement, shouting: "Say, what do you s'pose? Just now I was setting on my front door rock and I looked up the road and saw a buggy with a man and woman in it coming down the hill. But I couldn't see no hoss. And when they got down here to the bridge, BY GORRY, THE' WAN'T !NO HOSS! They went slippin' along down past the house just as slick. The man was steering the thing with a kind of crooked broom handle, and they was out of sight over in the Glen road in no time."

On that quiet summer Sunday morning twenty-eight years ago that strange new vehicle glided into the Glen along the way that ninety six years ago saw the coming of Dolly Copp's bridal "car." The occupants of that horseless buggy were Mr. and Mrs. F. O. Stanley, of Newton, Massachusetts. On that day, or a little later, in their Stanley steam motor, they made the first automobile ascent of Mount Washington. Not until four years later was an officially timed ascent made in one hour and forty-six minutes. In the next few years the "climbs to the clouds" of rival machines demonstrated the remarkable advancement of motor vehicles in speed and endurance. In 1901 that earliest record of one hour and forty-six minutes was reduced to a few seconds less than twenty-one minutes.

Today the jolting buckboard, the heavy mountain wagon, the gorgeous Concord coach, with its six prancing horses, no longer drag through the dust clouds of rutworn roads. Palatial touring cars by thousands glide along tarvia highways. Cars by hundreds park along the banks of the Peabody. The motor car possesses the Glen.

UNCLE SAM IN THE GLEN

At Washington on the morning of March 1, 1911, President Taft inaugurated a new era in the land of Dolly Copp by signing the long-delayed, long-fought-for and finally triumphant Weeks Bill for the purchase of forest reserves in the East. All honor to John W. Weeks, of Lancaster, New Hampshire, who saved the utility and beauty of the White Hills, saved the economic prosperity of New England, saved the grandeur of the Presidential Range for the health and joy of the people of the nation.

Two years later, under the authority of the Weeks Law, the Federal Government began the systematic purchase of forested areas in New Hampshire and Maine. The acquisition of tree-clad mountains has gone steadily on till, at the close of 1926, the National Forest possessed more than 441,000 acres. It is

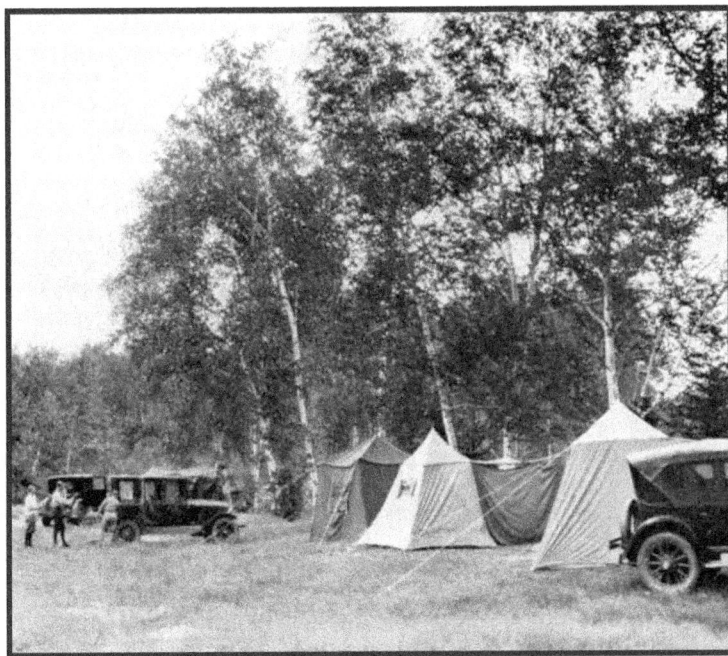

The Dolly Copp Campground

expected that this systematic expansion will go on till the White Mountain National Forest shall be a vast domain of a million acres, whose crowning glory will always be the peaks and ravines and scenic beauty of the Presidential Range from Webster to Madison, a panorama of regal monarchs that has no peer east of the Rockies. It is a nation's playground, to which a nation's people will resort each year in ever-increasing thousands.

In 1915 the Federal Government added to our National Forest the old farms in the Glen and laid out the Dolly Copp Camping Ground. Always extending the hospitable welcome of courteous officials, always in perfect sanitary condition, it is always the most popular and most populous of the Forest Service's public camping grounds.

The hospitality, the courtesy, the eternal vigilance of the National Forest officials are appreciated by the people who gather here day after day, and are teaching them precious lessons, deeper love for the beauty of Nature, better knowledge of the perils that beset that beauty. Under such teachings and in the atmosphere it creates, the fiend who plays fast and loose with fire, the assassin who assaults the defenseless tree with axe and knife, is seldom of this company.

Hither this summer will come more than six thousand of the summer vacationists to pitch their tents in Dolly Copp's fields, to gather the still blossoming flowers in Dolly's old-time garden, to drink from her crystal spring. At evening they will gather about the great fireplace to recount the simple, unconsciously heroic story of the Pioneers of the Glen, of *Daniel Pinkham,* of *Thomas Gulhane,* of *John Bellows,* and carry to their distant homes a kindly memory of *Hayes Dodifer* and

DOLLY COPP.